Veg[illegible]
Fast and Easy Sou[illegible] [illegible]pes
for Natural Weig[illegible] Loss and Detox

by **Vesela Tabakova**

Table Of Contents

Heart Warming Vegan Soups for all Seasons and Tastes

Our fast-paced lives leave us with less and less time for food planning and preparing healthy meals at home. When you don't have a lot of time to spend on dinner and all you want is to relax with your family, these simple and easy to cook vegan soups will allow you to get a great meal on the table that the whole family will love in an instant.

As a working mother of teenagers with mixed dietary preferences, I don't have the luxury of long periods in the kitchen and am constantly looking for new nutritious and varied vegan meals to add to my everyday menus. Here's a collection of some of my favorite ridiculously easy vegan soups that are perfect for a busy weeknight supper or a delicious weekend dinner.

Fresh Asparagus Soup

Serves: 4
Ingredients:

1 lb fresh asparagus, cut into pieces

1 small onion, chopped

3 garlic cloves, chopped

½ cup raw cashews, soaked in warm water for 1 hour

4 cups vegetable broth

2 tbsp olive oil

lemon juice, to taste

Directions:

Sauté onion for 3-4 minutes, stirring. Add in garlic and sauté for a minute more. Add in asparagus and sauté for 3-4 minutes.

Add broth, season with salt and pepper and bring to a boil then reduce heat and simmer for 20 minutes.

Set aside to cool, add cashews, and blend, until smooth. Season with lemon juice and serve.

Creamy Red Lentil Soup

Serves: 4
Ingredients:

1 cup red lentils

1/2 small onion, chopped

1 garlic clove, chopped

1 red pepper, chopped

2 cups water

1 can coconut milk

3 tbsp olive oil

1 tsp paprika

1/2 tsp ginger

salt and black pepper, to taste

Directions:

Heat olive oil in a large saucepan and sauté onion, garlic, red pepper, paprika, ginger and cumin, stirring. Add in red lentils and water. Bring to a boil, cover, and simmer for 20 minutes.

Add in coconut milk and simmer for 5 more minutes. Remove from heat, season with salt and black pepper, and blend until smooth.

Lentil, Barley and Kale Soup

Serves: 4
Ingredients:

2 medium leeks, chopped

2 garlic cloves, chopped

2 bay leaves

1 can tomatoes, diced and undrained

1/2 cup red lentils

1/2 cup barley

1 bunch kale, coarsely chopped

4 cups vegetable broth

3 tbsp olive oil

1 tbsp paprika

½ tsp cumin

Directions:

Heat olive oil in a large saucepan over medium-high heat and sauté leeks and garlic until fragrant. Add in cumin, paprika, tomatoes, lentils, barley and vegetable broth. Season with salt and pepper.

Cover and bring to a boil then reduce heat and simmer for 40 minutes or until barley is tender. Add in kale and let it simmer for a few minutes more until it wilts.

Spinach and Mushrooms Soup

Serves: 4-5
Ingredients:

1 small onion, finely cut

1 small carrot, chopped

1 small zucchini, diced

1 medium potato, diced

6-7 white mushrooms, chopped

2 cups chopped fresh spinach

4 cups vegetable broth or water

4 tbsp olive oil

salt and black pepper, to taste

Directions:

Heat olive oil in a large pot over medium heat. Add potato, onion and mushroom and cook until vegetables are soft but not mushy.

Add chopped fresh spinach, zucchini and vegetable broth and simmer for about 20 minutes. Season to taste with salt and pepper.

Broccoli and Potato Soup

Serves: 4-5
Ingredients:

1 lb broccoli, cut into florets

2 potatoes, chopped

1 onion, chopped

3 garlic cloves, crushed

4 cups water

2 tbsp olive oil

¼ tsp ground nutmeg

Directions:

Heat oil in a large saucepan over medium-high heat. Add onion and garlic and sauté, stirring, for 3 minutes, or until soft.

Add in broccoli, potato and 4 cups of cold water. Cover, bring to a boil, reduce heat and simmer, stirring, for 10-15 minutes, or until potatoes are tender.

Remove from heat and blend until smooth. Return to pan and cook until heated through. Season with nutmeg and black pepper before serving.

Moroccan Lentil Soup

Serves: 7-8
Ingredients:

1 cup red lentils

1 cup canned chickpeas, drained

1 onion, chopped

2 cloves garlic, minced

1 cup canned tomatoes, chopped

1 cup canned white beans, drained

3 carrots, diced

1 celery rib, diced

5 cups water

3 tbsp olive oil

1 tsp ginger, grated

1 tsp ground cardamom

1/2 tsp cumin

Directions:

In a large pot, sauté onions, garlic and ginger in olive oil for about 5 minutes. Add the water, lentils, chickpeas, white beans, tomatoes, carrots, celery, cardamom and cumin.

Bring to a boil for a few minutes, then simmer for half an hour or longer until the lentils are tender. Puree half the soup in a food processor or blender. Return the pureed soup to the pot, stir and serve.

Hearty Italian Minestrone

Serves: 4-5
Ingredients:

¼ head cabbage, chopped

2 carrots, chopped

1 celery rib, thinly sliced

1 small onion, chopped

2 garlic cloves, chopped

1 cup canned tomatoes, diced, undrained

1 cup fresh spinach, torn

1/2 cup pasta, cooked

3 cups water

2 tbsp olive oil

black pepper and salt, to taste

Directions:

Sauté the carrots, cabbage, celery, onion and garlic in oil for 5 minutes in a deep saucepan. Add water and tomatoes and bring to a boil.

Reduce heat and simmer uncovered, for 20 minutes, or until vegetables are tender. Stir in spinach, pasta, and season with pepper and salt to taste.

French Vegetable Soup

Serves: 6
Ingredients:

1 leek, thinly sliced

1 large zucchini, peeled and diced

1 cup green beans, halved

2 garlic cloves, chopped

1 cup canned tomatoes, chopped

3.5 oz vermicelli, broken into small pieces

3 cups vegetable broth

3 tbsp olive oil

black pepper, to taste

Directions:

Sauté the leek, zucchini, green beans and garlic for about 5 minutes, stirring. Add in the vegetable broth and tomatoes and bring to a boil then reduce heat.

Add black pepper to taste and simmer for 10 minutes or until the vegetables are tender but still holding their shape. Stir in the vermicelli. Cover again and simmer for a further 5 minutes. Serve warm.

Beetroot and Carrot Soup

Serves: 5-6
Ingredients:

4 beets, washed and peeled

2 carrots, peeled, chopped

2 potatoes, peeled, chopped

1 small onion, chopped

2 cups vegetable broth

2 cups water

3 tbsp olive oil

1 cup finely cut green onions, to serve

Directions:

Peel and chop the beets. Heat olive oil in a saucepan over medium-high heat and sauté the onion and carrot until tender. Add in beets, potatoes, broth and water. Bring to the boil then reduce heat and simmer, partially covered, for 30 minutes, or until beets are tender. Cool slightly.

Blend soup in batches until smooth. Return it to pan over low heat and cook, stirring, for 4-5 minutes, or until heated through. Season with salt and pepper. Serve sprinkled with green onions.

Celery, Apple and Carrot Soup

Serves: 4
Ingredients:

2 celery ribs, chopped

1 large apple, chopped

1/2 small onion, chopped

3 carrots, chopped

2 garlic cloves, crushed

4 cups vegetable broth

3 tbsp olive oil

1 tsp ginger powder

salt and black pepper, to taste

Directions:

Heat olive oil over medium-high heat and sauté onion, garlic, celery and carrots for 3-4 minutes, stirring. Add in ginger, apple and vegetable broth.

Bring to a boil then reduce heat and simmer, covered, for 10 minutes. Blend until smooth and return to the pot. Cook over medium-high heat until heated through. Season with salt and pepper to taste and serve.

Monastery Style White Bean Soup

Serves: 6-7
Ingredients:

2 cups white beans

2-3 carrots

1 large onion, finely chopped

1-2 tomatoes, grated

1 red bell pepper, chopped

1/2 cup finely cut fresh parsley

1 tbsp dried mint

1 tbsp paprika

¼ cup sunflower oil

salt, to taste

Directions:

Soak the beans in cold water for 3-4 hours or overnight, drain and discard the water.

Cover the beans with cold water. Add in oil, finely chopped carrots, onion and bell pepper.

Bring to a boil and simmer until the beans are tender. Add the grated tomatoes, mint, paprika and salt. Simmer for another 15 minutes. Serve sprinkled with finely chopped parsley.

Creamy Cauliflower Soup

Serves: 6-7
Ingredients:

1 onion, finely cut

1 medium head cauliflower, chopped

2-3 garlic cloves, minced

½ cup raw cashews, soaked in warm water for 1 hour

3 cups vegetable broth

1 cup coconut milk

¼ cup olive oil

salt, to taste

black pepper, to taste

Directions:

Heat the olive oil in a large pot over medium heat and gently sauté the onion, cauliflower and garlic. Stir in the vegetable broth and bring the mixture to a boil.

Reduce heat, cover, and simmer for 30 minutes. Remove the soup from heat, add in cashews, coconut milk, and blend in a blender or with a hand mixer. Season with salt and pepper to taste.

Pumpkin and Bell Pepper Soup

Serves: 4
Ingredients:

1 medium leek, chopped

9 oz pumpkin, peeled, deseeded, cut into small cubes

1/2 red bell pepper, cut into small pieces

1 can tomatoes, undrained, crushed

3 cups vegetable broth

1/2 tsp cumin

salt and black pepper, to taste

Directions:

Heat the olive oil in a medium saucepan and sauté the leek for 4-5 minutes. Add in the pumpkin and bell pepper and cook, stirring, for 5 minutes.

Add tomatoes, broth, and cumin and bring to a boil. Cover, reduce heat to low, and simmer, stirring occasionally, for 30 minutes or until vegetables are soft. Season with salt and pepper and leave aside to cool. Blend in batches and reheat to serve.

Creamy Potato Soup

Serves: 6-7
Ingredients:

4-5 medium potatoes, peeled and diced

2 carrots, chopped

1 zucchini, chopped

1 celery rib, chopped

5 cups water

3 tbsp olive oil

½ tsp dried rosemary

salt and black pepper, to taste

1/2 cup fresh parsley, finely cut

Directions:

Heat olive oil over medium heat and sauté the vegetables for 2-3 minutes. Add 4 cups of water, rosemary and bring the soup to a boil, then lower heat and simmer until all the vegetables are tender.

Blend soup in a blender until smooth. Serve warm, seasoned with black pepper and parsley sprinkled over each serving.

Shredded Cabbage Soup

Serves: 4-5
Ingredients:

1 onion, finely chopped

1 small cabbage, shredded

1 carrot, sliced

1 medium potato, peeled and diced

1 celery rib, sliced

2 tomatoes, diced

3 cups vegetable broth

3 tbsp sunflower oil

1 tsp cumin

salt, to taste

black pepper, to taste

Directions:

Heat sunflower oil over medium heat and gently sauté the onion for 2-3 minutes. Add in cabbage and sauté, stirring, for 2-3 minutes. Add carrots, potatoes, celery, tomatoes and cumin and stir again.

Add vegetable broth and bring the soup to a boil then reduce heat and simmer for 40 minutes. Season with salt and black pepper to taste.

Mediterranean Chickpea Soup

Serves: 7-8
Ingredients:

2 cups canned chickpeas, drained

1 onion, finely cut

2 cloves garlic, crushed

1 cup canned tomatoes, diced

6 cups vegetable broth

3 tbsp olive oil

1 bay leaf

½ tsp crushed rosemary

Directions:

Sauté onion and garlic in olive oil in a heavy soup pot. Add broth, chickpeas, tomato, bay leaf, and rosemary.

Bring to a boil then reduce heat and simmer for 30 minutes.

Wild Mushroom Soup

Serves: 4
Ingredients:

1 lb mixed wild mushrooms

1 onion, chopped

2 garlic cloves, crushed

1 tsp dried thyme

3 cups vegetable broth

3 tbsp olive oil

salt and pepper, to taste

Directions:

Sauté onions and garlic in a large soup pot until transparent. Add thyme and mushrooms.

Stir and cook for 10 minutes, then add vegetable broth and simmer for another 10-20 minutes. Blend, season and serve.

Spinach Soup

Serves: 4
Ingredients:

14 oz frozen spinach

1 large onion or 4-5 green onions

1 carrot, chopped

1/4 cup white rice

1-2 cloves garlic, cut

3 cups water

3-4 tbsp olive or sunflower oil

1 tsp paprika

black pepper, to taste

salt, to taste

Directions:

Heat oil in a cooking pot. Add the onion and carrot and sauté together for a few minutes, until just softened. Add chopped garlic, paprika and rice and stir for a minute. Remove from heat.

Add the spinach along with about 3 cups of hot water and season with salt and pepper. Bring back to the boil, then reduce the heat and simmer for around 30 minutes.

Tomato and Quinoa Soup

Serves: 4
Ingredients:

4 cups chopped fresh tomatoes or 2 cups canned tomatoes

1 large onion, diced

1/3 cup quinoa, washed very well

3 cups water

2 garlic cloves, minced

3 tbsp olive oil

1 tsp salt

½ tsp black pepper

1 tsp sugar

1 cup finely cut fresh parsley

Directions:

Sauté onions and garlic in olive oil in a large soup pot. When onions have softened, add tomatoes and water and bring to a boil. Lower heat and simmer for 5 minutes.

Blend the soup then return to the pot. Stir in quinoa and sugar and bring to a boil again, then reduce heat and simmer 15 minutes, stirring occasionally. Sprinkle with parsley and serve.

Spinach, Leek and Quinoa Soup

Serves: 4-5
Ingredients:

½ cup quinoa, very well washed

2 leeks halved lengthwise and sliced

1 onion, chopped

2 garlic cloves, chopped

1 can diced tomatoes, (15 oz), undrained

2 cups fresh spinach, cut

4 cups vegetable broth

2 tbsp olive oil

salt and pepper, to taste

Directions:

Heat olive oil in a large pot over medium heat and sauté onion for 2 minutes, stirring. Add leeks and cook for another 2-3 minutes, then add garlic and stir. Season with salt and black pepper to taste.

Add the vegetable broth, canned tomatoes and quinoa. Bring to a boil then reduce heat and simmer for 10 minutes. Stir in spinach and cook for another 5 minutes.

Vegetable Quinoa Soup

Serves: 6
Ingredients:

½ cup quinoa

1/2 onion, chopped

1 potato, diced

1 carrot, diced

1 red bell pepper, chopped

2 tomatoes, chopped

1 small zucchini, peeled and diced

4 cups water

1 tsp dried oregano

3-4 tbsp olive oil

black pepper, to taste

2 tbsp fresh lemon juice

Directions:

Rinse quinoa very well in a fine mesh strainer under running water; set aside to drain.

Heat the oil in a large soup pot and gently sauté the onions and carrot for 2-3 minutes, stirring every now and then. Add in potato, bell pepper, tomatoes, spices and water. Stir to combine.

Cover, bring to a boil, then lower heat and simmer for 10 minutes. Add in the quinoa and the zucchini; cover and simmer for 15 minutes or until the vegetables are tender. Add in the lemon juice; stir to combine and serve.

Roasted Brussels Sprouts and Cauliflower Soup

Serves 4
Ingredients:

1 onion, finely chopped

2 garlic cloves, crushed

16 oz cauliflower florets

16 oz Brussels sprouts, halved

4 cups vegetable broth

6 tbsp olive oil

salt and pepper, to taste

grated vegan cheese, to serve

Directions:

Preheat oven to 450F.

Line a large baking sheet and place the cauliflower and Brussels sprouts on it. Drizzle with half the olive oil and roast on the bottom third of the oven for 30 minutes, or until slightly browned.

Heat the remaining oil in a saucepan over medium heat and sauté the onion and garlic, stirring, for 2-3 minutes or until soft.

Add in vegetable broth and bring to the boil then simmer 3-4 minutes. Stir in roasted vegetables and cook for 5 minutes more.

Set aside to cool then blend in batches and reheat. Serve sprinkled with cheese.

Roasted Brussels Sprouts and Sweet Potato Soup

Serves 4
Ingredients:

1 onion, finely chopped

2 garlic cloves, crushed

2 carrots, chopped

1 large sweet potatoes, peeled and chopped

16 oz Brussels sprouts, shredded

4 cups vegetable broth

4 tbsp olive oil

1 tsp paprika

1 tsp dried oregano

salt and pepper, to taste

Directions:

Preheat oven to 450F.

Line a large baking sheet and place the Brussels sprouts on it. Drizzle with half the olive oil and season with salt and pepper to taste. Roast on the bottom third of the oven for 20 minutes, or until golden.

In a saucepan, heat the remaining oil over medium heat and sauté the onion, carrots, and garlic, stirring, for 2-3 minutes or until soft. Add paprika and stir to combine.

Add in the vegetable broth, sweet potatoes and oregano. Bring to the boil then simmer 15 minutes or until vegetables are tender.

Stir in roasted Brussels sprouts and cook for 5 minutes more.

Broccoli and Zucchini Soup

Serves 4-5
Ingredients:

2 leeks, white part only, sliced

1 head broccoli, coarsely chopped

2 zucchinis, peeled and chopped

1 potato, peeled and chopped

2 cups vegetable broth

3 cups water

3 tbsp olive oil

1/3 cup coconut milk

salt and pepper, to taste

Directions:

Heat the oil in a large saucepan over medium heat. Sauté the leeks, stirring, for 5 minutes or until soft.

Add in bite sized pieces of broccoli, zucchinis and potato. Stir in the water and broth and bring to a boil.

Reduce heat to low and simmer, stirring occasionally, for 15 minutes, or until vegetables are just tender. Remove from heat and set aside for 5 minutes to cool slightly.

Transfer soup to a blender and blend in batches until smooth. Return to saucepan and place over low heat. Add milk and stir to combine. Season with salt and pepper to taste.

Baked Beet and Apple Soup

Serves 4-5
Ingredients:

1.5 lb fresh beets, peeled and grated

2 carrots, chopped

1 onion, chopped

2 apples, peeled and chopped

1 tbsp sugar

1 bay leaf

2 tbs lemon juice

3 cups vegetable broth

3 tbsp olive oil

a bunch of fresh parsley, chopped, to serve

salt and black pepper, to taste

Directions:

Preheat the oven to 350 F. Toss the beets, apples, onion and carrots in olive oil and arrange in a casserole dish.

Add in the bay leaf and vegetable broth. Season with salt and pepper, cover with foil and bake for 1-2 hours. Discard the bay leaf and set aside to cool.

Blend everything in a blender, in batches, until smooth, then transfer to a large saucepan.

Season with salt and pepper to taste and reheat without boiling. Serve the soup sprinkled with chopped parsley.

Vegetarian Borscht

Serves 6
Ingredients:

4 beets, peeled, quartered

1 carrot, peeled, chopped

1 parsnip, peeled, cut into chunks

1 leek, white part only, sliced

1 onion, chopped

1/3 cup lemon juice

½ tsp nutmeg

3 bay leaves

6 cups vegetable broth

2-3 dill springs, chopped

Directions:

Place the beets, carrot, parsnip, leek, onion, lemon juice, spices and bay leaves in a large saucepan with the vegetable broth.

Bring to the boil, then reduce the heat to low and simmer, partially covered, for 1 ½ hours.

Cool slightly, then blend in batches and season well with salt and pepper. Return to the saucepan and gently heat through. Place in bowls and garnish with dill.

Spiced Parsnip Soup

Serves 4
Ingredients:

1.5 lb parsnips, peeled, chopped

2 onions, chopped

1 garlic clove

3 tbsp olive oil

1 tbs curry powder

salt and freshly ground pepper, to taste

Directions:

Sauté the onion and garlic together with the curry powder in a large saucepan. Stir in the parsnips and cook, stirring often, for 10 minutes.

Add in 5 cups of water, bring to the boil, and simmer for 30 minutes, or until the parsnips are tender.

Set aside to cool, then blend in batches until smooth. Season with salt and pepper.

Pumpkin and Chickpea Soup

Serves 6
Ingredients:

1 leek, white part only, thinly sliced

3 cloves garlic, finely chopped

2 carrots, peeled, coarsely chopped

2 lb pumpkin, peeled, deseeded, diced

1/3 cup chickpeas

½ tsp ground ginger

½ tsp ground cinnamon

½ tsp ground cumin

5 tbsp olive oil

Juice of ½ lemon

parsley springs, to serve

Directions:

Heat oil in a large saucepan and sauté leek, garlic and 2 tsp salt, stirring occasionally, until soft. Add cinnamon, ginger and cumin and stir. Add in carrots, pumpkin and chickpeas.

Add 5 cups of water to saucepan and bring to the boil, then reduce heat and simmer for 50 minutes or until the chickpeas are soft.

Remove from heat, add lemon juice and blend soup, in batches, until smooth. Return it to pan over low heat and cook, stirring, for 4-5 minutes, or until heated through. Serve topped with parsley sprigs.

Brussels Sprouts and Potato Soup

Serves 4-5
Ingredients:

16 oz Brussels sprouts

2 potatoes, peeled and chopped

1 onion, chopped

3 garlic cloves, crushed

4 cups water

2 tbsp olive oil

salt and black pepper, to taste

Directions:

Heat oil in a large saucepan over medium-high heat. Add onion and garlic and sauté, stirring, for 1-2 minutes until fragrant.

Add in Brussels sprouts, potatoes, rosemary and 4 cups of vegetable broth.

Cover and bring to the boil, then reduce heat to low. Simmer for 30 minutes, or until potatoes are tender.

Remove from heat. Blend until smooth. Return to pan. Cook for 4-5 minutes or until heated through. Season with salt and pepper and serve.

Brussels Sprouts and Tomato Soup

Serves 4-5
Ingredients:

16 oz Brussels sprouts

4 large tomatoes, diced

1 medium onion, chopped

3 garlic cloves, crushed

1 tsp sugar

2 cups vegetable broth

1 tbsp paprika

2 tbsp olive oil

salt and black pepper, to taste

Directions:

Heat oil in a deep soup pot over medium-high heat. Add onion, garlic and paprika and sauté, stirring, for 2-3 minutes or until soft.

Add in tomatoes and vegetable broth. Cover and bring to the boil, then reduce heat to low and simmer, stirring, for 10 minutes.

Remove from heat and blend until smooth. Return to pan. Stir in Brussels sprouts. Cook for 15 minutes more. Season with salt and pepper before serving.

Leek, Rice and Potato Soup

Serves 4-5
Ingredients:

1/3 cup rice

4 cups of water

2-3 potatoes, peeled and diced

1 small onion, cut

1 leek halved lengthwise and sliced

3 tbsp olive oil

lemon juice, to serve

Directions:

Heat a soup pot over medium heat. Add olive oil and onion and sauté for 2 minutes. Add leeks and potatoes and cook for a few minutes more.

Add three cups of water, bring to a boil, reduce heat and simmer for 5 minutes. Add the very well washed rice and simmer for 10 minutes. Serve with lemon juice to taste.

Lightly Spiced Carrot and Chickpea Soup

Serves 4-5
Ingredients:

3-4 big carrots, chopped

1 leek, chopped

4 cups vegetable broth

1 cup canned chickpeas, undrained

½ cup orange juice

2 tbsp olive oil

½ tsp cumin

½ tsp ginger

Directions:

Heat oil in a large saucepan over medium heat. Add in the leek and carrots and sauté until soft. Add orange juice, broth, chickpeas and spices.

Bring to the boil. Reduce heat to medium-low and simmer, covered, for 15 minutes. Blend soup until smooth, return to pan. Season with salt and pepper. Stir over heat until heated through. Pour in 4-5 bowls and serve.

Carrot and Ginger Soup

Serves 4
Ingredients:

6 carrots, peeled and chopped

1 medium onion, chopped

4 cups water

3 tbsp olive oil

2 cloves garlic, minced

1 tbsp grated ginger

½ bunch fresh coriander, finely cut

salt and black pepper, to taste

Directions:

Heat the olive oil in a large pot over medium heat and sauté the onions, carrots, garlic and ginger until tender. Add in water and bring to a boil.

Reduce heat to low and simmer 30 minutes. Transfer the soup to a blender or food processor and blend, until smooth. Return to the pot and continue cooking for a few more minutes.

Remove soup from heat and serve with coriander sprinkled over each serving.

Sweet Potato Soup

Serves 6-7
Ingredients:

2 lb sweet potato, peeled, chopped

1 lb potatoes, peeled chopped

1 medium onions, chopped

4 cups vegetable broth

5 tbsp olive oil

2 cloves garlic, minced

1 red chili pepper, finely chopped

salt and pepper, to taste

Directions:

Heat the olive oil in a large pot over medium heat and sauté the onions, garlic and chili pepper until just fragrant. Add the potatoes and sweet potatoes and add in the broth. Bring to a boil.

Reduce heat to low and simmer 30 minutes or until potatoes are tender. Transfer the soup to a blender or food processor and blend, until smooth. Return to the pot and continue cooking for a few more minutes. Remove soup from heat and serve.

Irish Carrot Soup

Serves 5-6
Ingredients:

5-6 carrots, peeled, chopped

2 potatoes, peeled, chopped

1 small onion, chopped

4 cups vegetable broth

3 tbsp olive oil

salt and pepper, to taste

Directions:

Heat olive oil in a deep saucepan over medium-high heat and sauté the onion and carrot until tender. Add in potatoes and vegetable broth.

Bring to the boil then reduce heat and simmer, partially covered, for 30 minutes, or until carrots are tender.

Set aside to cool then blend in batches until smooth. Return soup to saucepan and cook, stirring, for 4-5 minutes, or until heated through. Season with salt and pepper and serve.

Lentil, Buckwheat and Mushroom Soup

Serves 4-5
Ingredients:

2 medium leeks, trimmed, halved, sliced

10 white mushrooms, sliced

1/2 cup buckwheat groats (use either raw or toasted), rinsed

3 garlic cloves, cut

2 bay leaves

2 cans tomatoes chopped, undrained

3/4 cup red lentils

1/2 cup buckwheat groats (use either raw or toasted), rinsed

3 tbsp olive oil

1 tsp paprika

1 tsp oregano

½ tsp cumin

salt and pepper, to taste

Directions:

Heat the oil in a large saucepan over medium-high heat. Gently sauté the leeks and mushrooms for 3-4 minutes or until softened. Add in cumin, paprika, oregano and tomatoes, lentils, buckwheat, and 5 cups of cold water. Season with salt and pepper.

Cover and bring to the boil. Reduce heat to low. Simmer for 35-40 minutes, or until the buckwheat is tender.

Minted Pea and Potato Soup

Serves 4
Ingredients:

1 onion, finely chopped

2 garlic cloves, finely chopped

4 cups vegetable broth

3-4 large potatoes, peeled and diced

1 lb green peas, frozen

1/3 cup mint leaves

3 tbsp olive oil

small mint leaves, to serve

Directions:

Heat oil in a large saucepan over medium-high heat and sauté onion and garlic for 5 minutes or until soft.

Add vegetable broth and bring to the boil, then add potatoes and mint. Cover, reduce heat, and cook for 15 minutes until tender. Add the peas 2 min before the end of the cooking time.

Remove from heat. Set aside to cool slightly, then blend soup, in batches, until smooth.

Return soup to saucepan over medium-low heat and cook until heated through. Season with salt and pepper.

Serve topped with mint leaves.

Brussels Sprout and Lentil Soup

Serves 4
Ingredients:

1 cup brown lentils

1 onion, chopped

2-3 cloves garlic, peeled

2 medium carrots, chopped

16 oz Brussels sprouts, shredded

4 cups vegetable broth

4 tbsp olive oil

1 ½ tsp paprika

1 tsp summer savory

Directions:

Heat oil in a deep soup pot, add the onion and carrots and sauté until golden. Add in paprika and lentils with vegetable broth.

Bring to the boil, lower heat and simmer for 15-20 minutes. Add the Brussels sprouts and the tomato to the soup, together with the garlic and summer savory. Cook for 15 more minutes, add salt to taste and serve.

Curried Lentil Soup

Serves 5-6
Ingredients:

1 cup dried lentils

1 large onion, finely cut

1 celery rib, chopped

1 large carrot, chopped

3 garlic cloves, chopped

1 can tomatoes, undrained

3 cups vegetable broth

1 tbsp curry powder

1/2 tsp ground ginger

Directions:

Combine all ingredients in slow cooker.

Cover and cook on low for 5-6 hours.

Blend soup to desired consistency, adding additional hot water to thin, if desired.

Green Lentil Soup with Rice

Serves 6
Ingredients:

1 cup green lentils

1 small onion, finely cut

1 carrot, chopped

5 cups vegetable broth

1/4 cup rice

1 tbsp paprika

salt and black pepper, to taste

1/2 cup finely cut dill, to serve

Directions:

Heat oil in a large saucepan and sauté the onion stirring occasionally, until transparent. Add in carrot, paprika and lentils and stir to combine.

Add vegetable broth to the saucepan and bring to the boil, then reduce heat and simmer for 20 minutes.

Stir in rice and cook on medium low until rice is cooked. Sprinkle with dill and serve.

Simple Black Bean Soup

Serves 5-6
Ingredients:

1 cup dried black beans

5 cups vegetable broth

1 large onion, chopped

1 red pepper, chopped

1 tsp sweet paprika

1 tbsp dried mint

2 bay leaves

1 Serrano chili, finely chopped

1 tsp salt

4 tbsp fresh lime juice

1/2 cup chopped fresh cilantro

1 cup vegan cream, to serve

Directions:

Wash the beans and soak them in enough water overnight.

In a slow cooker, combine the beans and all other ingredients except for the lime juice and cilantro. Cover and cook on low for 7-8 hours.

Add salt, lime juice and fresh cilantro.

Serve with a dollop of vegan cream.

Bean and Pasta Soup

Serves 6-7
Ingredients:

1 cup small pasta, cooked

1 cup canned white beans, rinsed and drained

2 medium carrots, cut

1 cup fresh spinach, torn

1 medium onion, chopped

1 celery rib, chopped

2 garlic cloves, crushed

3 cups water

1 cup canned tomatoes, diced and undrained

1 cup vegetable broth

½ tsp rosemary

½ tsp basil

salt and pepper, to taste

Directions:

Add all ingredients except pasta and spinach into slow cooker. Cover and cook on low for 6-7 hours or high for 4 hours.

Add spinach and pasta about 30 minutes before the soup is finished cooking.

Slow Cooked Split Pea Soup

Serves 5-6
Ingredients:

1 lb dried green split peas, rinsed and drained

2 potatoes, peeled and diced

1 small onion, chopped

1 celery rib, chopped

1 carrot, chopped

2 garlic cloves, chopped

1 bay leaf

1 tsp black pepper

1/2 tsp salt

6 cups water

Directions:

Combine all ingredients in slow cooker.

Cover and cook on low for 5-6 hours.

Discard bay leaf. Blend soup to desired consistency, adding additional hot water to thin, if desired.

Serve with garlic or herb bread.

Spiced Citrus Bean Soup

Serves 6-7
Ingredients:

1 can (14 oz) white beans, rinsed and drained

2 medium carrots, cut

1 medium onion, chopped

1 tbsp gram masala

4 cups vegetable broth

1 cup coconut milk

1/2 tbsp grated ginger

juice of 1 orange

salt and pepper, to taste

1/2 cup fresh parsley leaves, finely cut, to serve

Directions:

In a large soup pot, sauté onions, carrots and ginger in olive oil, for about 5 minutes, stirring. Add gram masala and cook until just fragrant.

Add the orange juice and vegetable broth and bring to the boil. Simmer for about 10 min until the carrots are tender, then stir in the coconut milk.

Blend soup to desired consistency then add the beans and bring to a simmer. Serve sprinkled with parsley.

Slow Cooker Tuscan-style Soup

Serves 5-6
Ingredients:

1 lb potatoes, peeled and cubed

1 small onion, chopped

1 can mixed beans, drained

1 carrot, chopped

2 garlic cloves, chopped

4 cups vegetable broth

1 cups chopped kale

3 tbsp olive oil

1 bay leaf

salt and pepper, to taste

Grated vegan cheese, to serve

Directions:

Heat oil in a skillet over medium heat and sauté the onion, carrot and garlic, stirring, for 2-3 minutes or until soft.

Combine all ingredients except the kale into the slow cooker. Season with salt and pepper to taste.

Cook on high for 4 hours or low for 6-7 hours. Add in kale about 30 minutes before soup is finished cooking. Serve sprinkled with vegan cheese.

Creamy Artichoke Soup

Serves 4
Ingredients:

1 can artichoke hearts, drained

3 cups vegetable broth

2 tbsp lemon juice

1 small onion, finely cut

2 cloves garlic, crushed

3 tbsp olive oil

2 tbsp flour

½ cup vegan cream

Directions:

Gently sauté the onion and garlic in some olive oil. Add the flour, whisking constantly, and then add the hot vegetable broth slowly, while still whisking. Cook for about 5 minutes.

Blend the artichoke, lemon juice, salt and pepper until smooth. Add the puree to the broth mix, stir well, and then stir in the cream. Cook until heated through. Garnish with a swirl of vegan cream or a sliver of artichoke.

Tomato Artichoke Soup

Serves 4
Ingredients:

1 can artichoke hearts, drained

1 can diced tomatoes, undrained

3 cups vegetable broth

1 small onion, chopped

2 cloves garlic, crushed

1 tbsp pesto

black pepper, to taste

Directions:

Combine all ingredients in the slow cooker.

Cover and cook on low for 8-10 hours or on high for 4-5 hours.

Blend the soup in batches and return it to the slow cooker. Season with salt and pepper to taste and serve.

Creamy Artichoke and Horseradish Soup

Serves 4
Ingredients:

1 can artichoke hearts, drained

3 cups vegetable broth

1 tbsp vegan horseradish sauce

2 tbsp lemon juice

1 small onion, finely cut

2 cloves garlic, crushed

3 tbsp olive oil

2 tbsp flour

2 tbsp chopped fresh chives plus extra to garnish

Directions:

Gently sauté the onion and garlic in some olive oil. Add in the flour, whisking constantly, and then add the hot vegetable broth slowly, while still whisking. Cook for about 5 minutes.

Blend the artichokes, salt and pepper until smooth. Add the puree to the broth mix, stir well, and then stir in the horseradish sauce and chopped chives.

Ladle the soup into bowls and serve.

Roasted Red Pepper Soup

Serves 5-6
Ingredients:

5-6 large red peppers

1 large onion, chopped

2 garlic cloves, crushed

4 medium tomatoes, chopped

4 cups vegetable broth

3 tbsp olive oil

2 bay leaves

Directions:

Grill the peppers or roast them in the oven at 400 F until the skins are a little burnt. Place the roasted peppers in a brown paper bag or a lidded container and leave covered for about 10 minutes. This makes it easier to peel them. Peel the skins and remove the seeds. Cut the peppers in small pieces.

Heat oil in a large saucepan over medium-high heat. Add onion and garlic and sauté, stirring, for 3 minutes or until onion has softened. Add the red peppers, bay leaves, tomato and simmer for 5 minutes.

Add broth. Season with pepper. Bring to the boil, then reduce heat and simmer for 20 more minutes. Set aside to cool slightly. Blend, in batches, until smooth and serve.

Vietnamese Noodle Soup

Serves 4
Ingredients:

9 oz rice stick noodles

4 cups vegetable broth

1 lemongrass stem, only pale part, finely chopped

2 garlic cloves, cut

½ tsp ground ginger

1 long red chili, thinly sliced

3.5 oz shiitake mushrooms

1 cup bean sprouts

4 tbsp lime juice

coriander and mint leaves, to garnish

Directions:

Pour boiling water over the noodles and leave aside for 10 minutes, or until soft. Place the vegetable broth, lemongrass, garlic, ginger, chili and 3 cups of water in a large saucepan.

Bring to the boil, then reduce heat to medium. Simmer for 10 minutes. Add in mushrooms and cook for 5 more minutes, then stir in the lime juice. Divide the noodles and bean sprouts among bowls. Serve the soup topped with coriander and mint leaves.

Celery Root Soup

Serves 4
Ingredients:

2 leeks (white and light green parts only), chopped

2 garlic cloves, crushed

1 large celery root, peeled and diced

2 potatoes, peeled and diced

4 cups vegetable broth

1 bay leaf

2 tbsp olive oil

salt and black pepper, to taste

Directions:

In a skillet, heat olive oil, then add the leeks and sauté about 3-4 minutes. Add in the garlic and sauté an additional 3-40 seconds.

In a slow cooker, add the sautéed leeks and garlic, celeriac, potatoes, broth, bay leaf, salt, and pepper. Cover and cook on low heat for 7-8 hours. Set aside to cool, remove the bay leaf, then process in a blender or with an immersion blender until smooth.

Quinoa, White Bean, and Kale Soup

Serves 5-6
Ingredients:

½ cup uncooked quinoa, rinsed well

1 small onion, chopped

1 can diced tomatoes, undrained

2 cans cannellini beans, undrained

3 cups chopped kale

2 garlic cloves, chopped

4 cups vegetable broth

1 tsp paprika

1 tsp dried mint

salt and pepper, to taste

Directions:

Combine all ingredients except the kale into the slow cooker. Season with salt and pepper to taste.

Cook on high for 4 hours or low for 6-7 hours. Add in kale about 30 minutes before soup is finished cooking.

FREE BONUS RECIPES: 10 Ridiculously Easy Jam and Jelly Recipes Anyone Can Make

A Different Strawberry Jam

Makes 6-7 11 oz jars
Ingredients:

4 lb fresh small strawberries (stemmed and cleaned)

5 cups sugar

1 cup water

2 tbsp lemon juice or 1 tsp citric acid

Directions:

Mix water and sugar and bring to the boil. Simmer sugar syrup for 5-6 minutes then slowly drop in the cleaned strawberries. Stir and bring to the boil again. Lower heat and simmer, stirring and skimming any foam off the top once or twice.

Drop a small amount of the jam on a plate and wait a minute to see if it has thickened. If it has gelled enough, turn off the heat. If not, keep boiling and test every 5 minutes until ready. Two or three minutes before you remove the jam from the heat, add lemon juice or citric acid and stir well.

Ladle the hot jam in the jars until 1/8-inch from the top. Place the lid on top and flip the jar upside down. Continue until all of the jars are filled and upside down. Allow the jam to cool completely before turning right-side up. Press on the lid to check and see if it has sealed. If one of the jars lids doesn't pop up- the jar is not sealed–store it in a refrigerator.

Raspberry Jam

Makes 4-5 11 oz jars
Ingredients:

4 cups raspberries

4 cups sugar

1 tsp vanilla extract

1/2 tsp citric acid

Directions:

Gently wash and drain the raspberries. Lightly crush them with a potato masher, food mill or a food processor. Do not puree, it is better to have bits of fruit. Sieve half of the raspberry pulp to remove some of the seeds. Combine sugar and raspberries in a wide, thick-bottomed pot and bring mixture to a full rolling boil, stirring constantly. Skim any scum or foam that rises to the surface. Boil until the jam sets.

Test by putting a small drop on a cold plate – if the jam is set, it will wrinkle when given a small poke with your finger. Add citric acid, vanilla, and stir. Simmer for 2-3 minutes more, then ladle into hot jars. Flip upside down or process 10 minutes in boiling water.

Raspberry-Peach Jam

Makes 4-5 11 oz jars
Ingredients:

2 lb peaches

1 1/2 cup raspberries

4 cups sugar

1 tsp citric acid

Directions:

Wash and slice the peaches. Clean the raspberries and combine them with the peaches is a wide, heavy-bottomed saucepan. Cover with sugar and set aside for a few hours or overnight. Bring the fruit and sugar to a boil over medium heat, stirring occasionally. Remove any foam that rises to the surface.

Boil until the jam sets. Add citric acid and stir. Simmer for 2-3 minutes more, then ladle into hot jars. Flip upside down or process 10 minutes in boiling water.

Blueberry Jam

Makes 4-5 11 oz jars
Ingredients:

4 cups granulated sugar

3 cups blueberries (frozen and thawed or fresh)

3/4 cup honey

2 tbsp lemon juice

1 tsp lemon zest

Directions:

Gently wash and drain the blueberries. Lightly crush them with a potato masher, food mill or a food processor. Add the honey, lemon juice, and lemon zest, then bring to a boil over medium-high heat. Boils for 10-15 minutes, stirring from time to time. Boil until the jam sets.

Test by putting a small drop on a cold plate – if the jam is set, it will wrinkle when given a small poke with your finger. Skim off any foam, then ladle the jam into jars. Seal, flip upside down or process for 10 minutes in boiling water.

Triple Berry Jam

Makes 4-5 11 oz jars
Ingredients:

1 cup strawberries

1 cup raspberries

2 cups blueberries

4 cups sugar

1 tsp citric acid

Directions:

Mix berries and add sugar. Set aside for a few hours or overnight. Bring the fruit and sugar to the boil over medium heat, stirring frequently. Remove any foam that rises to the surface. Boil until the jam sets. Add citric acid, salt and stir.

Simmer for 2-3 minutes more, then ladle into hot jars. Flip upside down or process 10 minutes in boiling water.

Red Currant Jelly

Makes 6-7 11 oz jars
Ingredients:

2 lb fresh red currants

1/2 cup water

3 cups sugar

1 tsp citric acid

Directions:

Place the currants into a large pot, and crush with a potato masher or berry crusher. Add in water, and bring to a boil. Simmer for 10 minutes. Strain the fruit through a jelly or cheese cloth and measure out 4 cups of the juice. Pour the juice into a large saucepan, and stir in the sugar. Bring to full rolling boil, then simmer for 20-30 minutes, removing any foam that may rise to the surface. When the jelly sets, ladle in hot jars, flip upside down or process in boiling water for 10 minutes.

White Cherry Jam

Makes 3-4 11 oz jars
Ingredients:

2 lb cherries

3 cups sugar

2 cups water

1 tsp citric acid

Directions:

Wash and stone cherries. Combine water and sugar and bring to the boil. Boil for 5-6 minutes then remove from heat and add cherries. Bring to a rolling boil and cook until set. Add citric acid, stir and boil 1-2 minutes more.

Ladle in hot jars, flip upside down or process in boiling water for 10 minutes.

Cherry Jam

Makes 3-4 11 oz jars
Ingredients:

2 lb fresh cherries, pitted, halved

4 cups sugar

1/2 cup lemon juice

Directions:

Place the cherries in a large saucepan. Add sugar and set aside for an hour. Add the lemon juice and place over low heat. Cook, stirring occasionally, for 10 minutes or until sugar dissolves. Increase heat to high and bring to a rolling boil.

Cook for 5-6 minutes or until jam is set. Remove from heat and ladle hot jam into jars, seal and flip upside down.

Oven Baked Ripe Figs Jam

Makes 3-4 11 oz jars
Ingredients:

2 lb ripe figs

2 cups sugar

1 ½ cups water

2 tbsp lemon juice

Directions:

Arrange the figs in a Dutch oven, if they are very big, cut them in halves. Add sugar and water and stir well. Bake at 350 F for about one and a half hours. Do not stir. You can check the readiness by dropping a drop of the syrup in a cup of cold water – if it falls to the bottom without dissolving, the jam is ready. If the drop dissolves before falling, you can bake it a little longer. Take out of the oven, add lemon juice and ladle in the warm jars. Place the lids on top and flip the jars upside down. Allow the jam to cool completely before turning right-side up.

If you want to process the jams - place them into a large pot, cover the jars with water by at least 2 inches and bring to a boil. Boil for 10 minutes, remove the jars and sit to cool.

Quince Jam

Makes 5-6 11 oz jars
Ingredients:

4 lb quinces

5 cups sugar

2 cups water

1 tsp lemon zest

3 tbsp lemon juice

Directions:

Combine water and sugar in a deep, thick-bottomed saucepan and bring it to the boil. Simmer, stirring until the sugar has completely dissolved. Rinse the quinces, cut in half, and discard the cores. Grate the quinces, using a cheese grater or a blender to make it faster. Quince flesh tends to darken very quickly, so it is good to do this as fast as possible.

Add the grated quinces to the sugar syrup and cook uncovered, stirring occasionally until the jam turns pink and thickens to desired consistency, about 40 minutes. Drop a small amount of the jam on a plate and wait a minute to see if it has thickened. If it has gelled enough, turn off the heat. If not, keep boiling and test every 2-3 minutes until ready.

Two or three minutes before you remove the jam from the heat, add lemon juice and lemon zest and stir well.

Ladle in hot, sterilized jars and flip upside down.

About the Author

Vesela lives in Bulgaria with her family of six (including the Jack Russell Terrier). Her passion is going green in everyday life and she loves to prepare homemade cosmetic and beauty products for all her family and friends.
Vesela has been publishing her cookbooks for over a year now. If you want to see other healthy family recipes that she has published, together with some natural beauty books, you can check out her Author Page on Amazon.

Before You Go

Thank you for purchasing my book and trying out my recipes! If you enjoyed my vegan soups, please consider leaving a review at Amazon, even if it's only a line or two; it would be really appreciated.

Made in the
USA
Middletown, DE